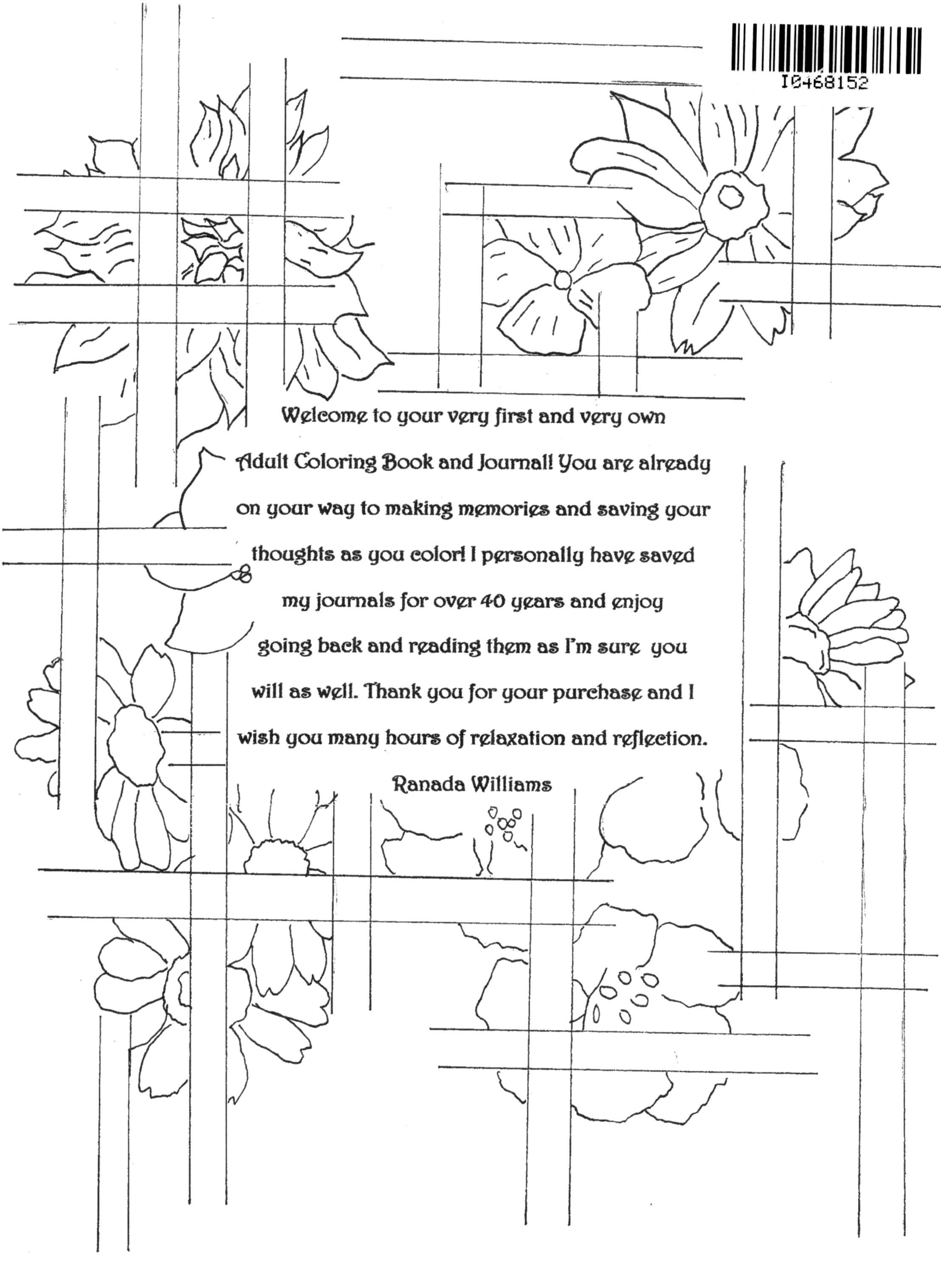

Welcome to your very first and very own Adult Coloring Book and Journal! You are already on your way to making memories and saving your thoughts as you color! I personally have saved my journals for over 40 years and enjoy going back and reading them as I'm sure you will as well. Thank you for your purchase and I wish you many hours of relaxation and reflection.

Ranada Williams

Journaling can provide you having something to leave behind with your children to tell your life story.

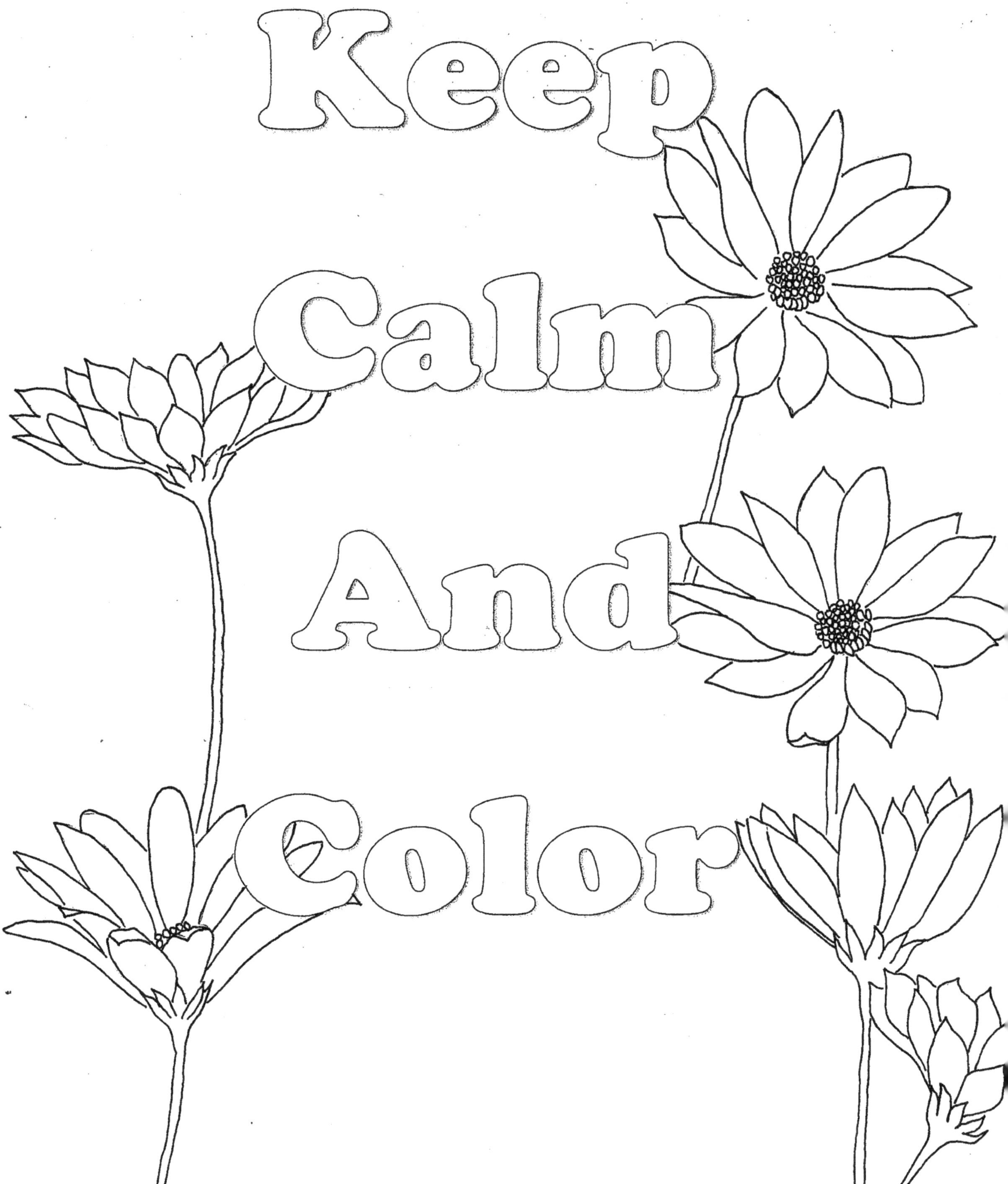
Keep
Calm
And
Color

Listening to a fountain or a rain storm can be relaxing.

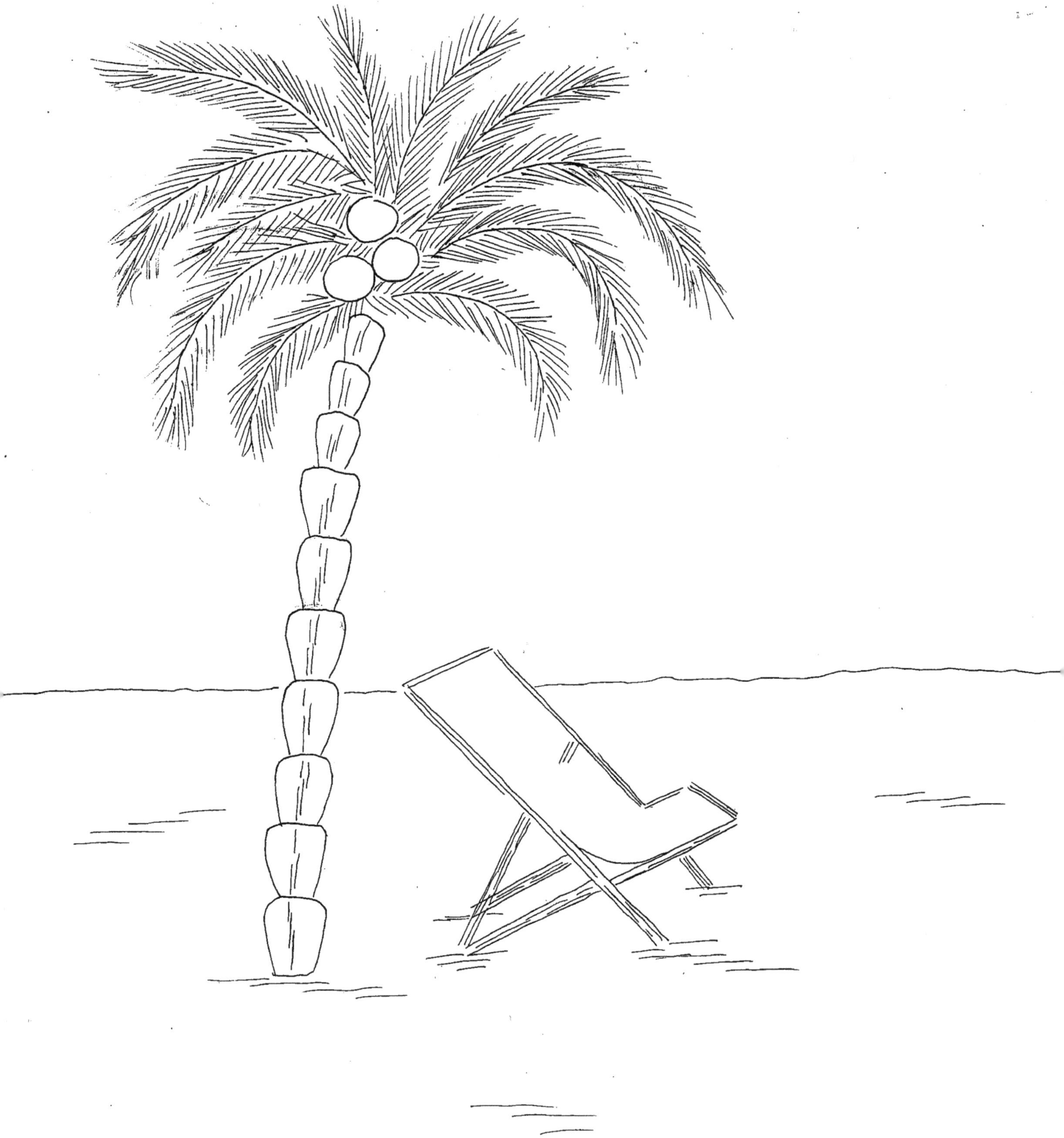

When we are stressed we do not breathe as much oxygen as we need.

From the 1440 minutes in a day, take 14 to relax.

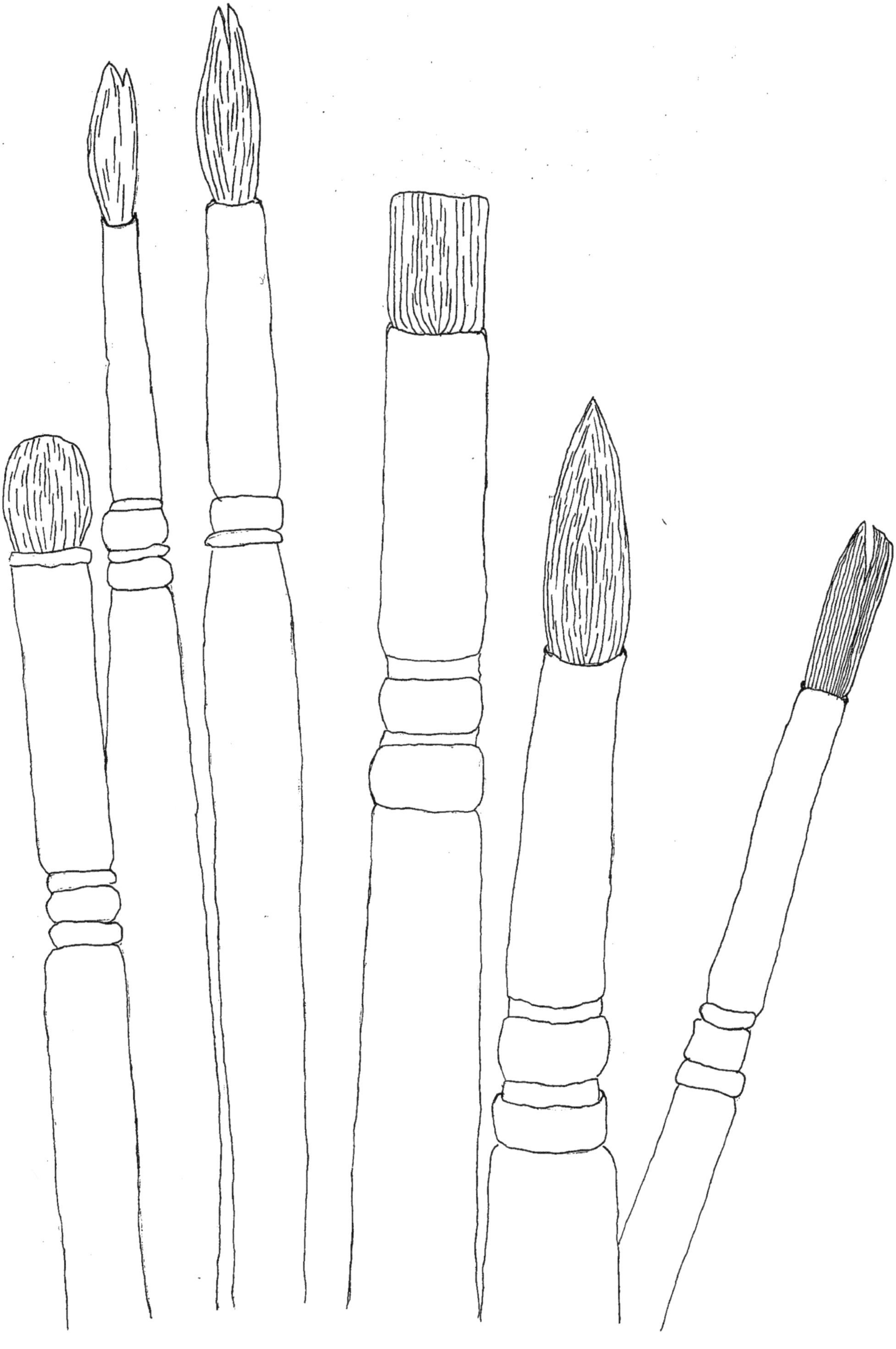

Relaxing boosts your memory.

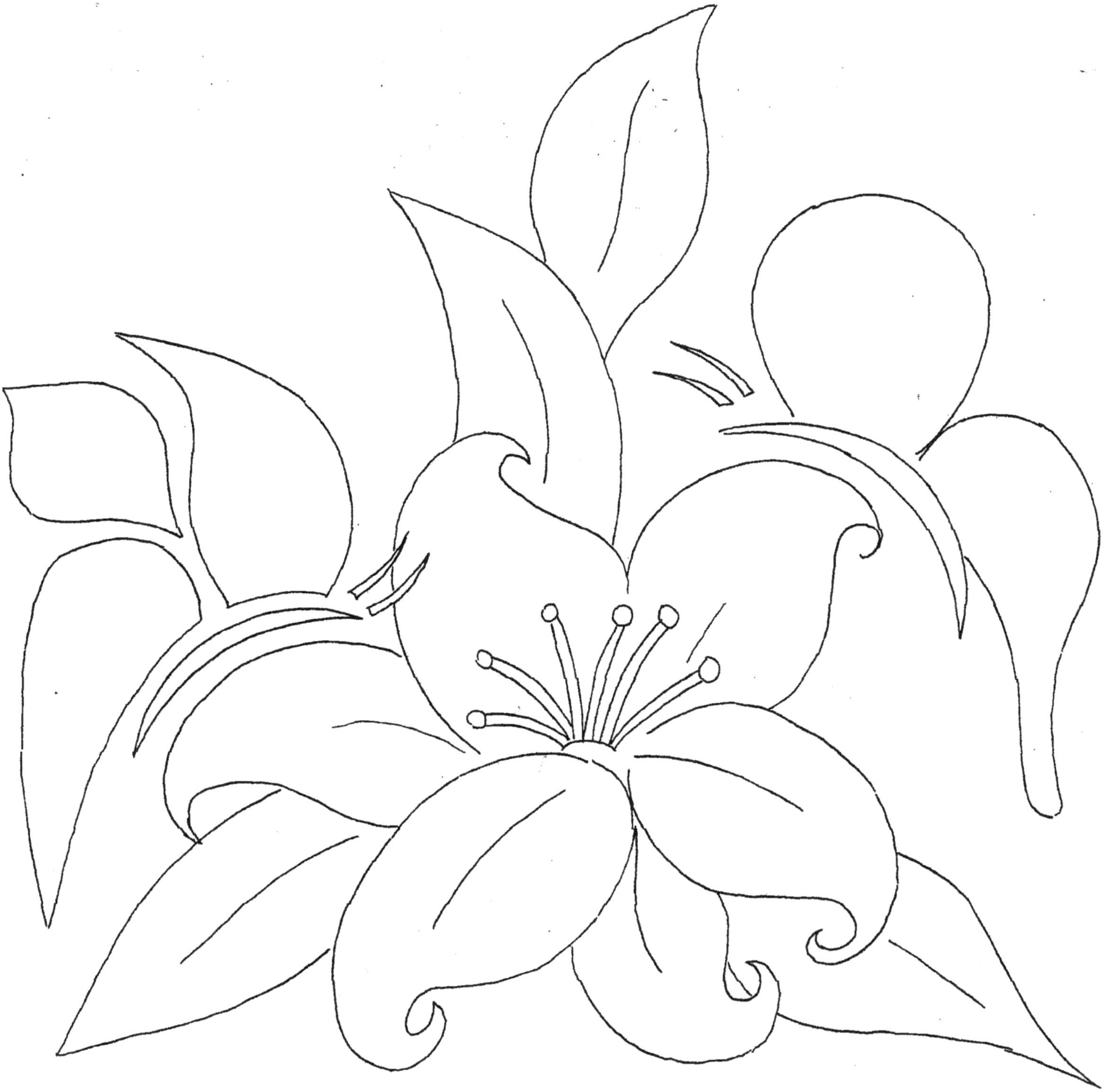

Cuddling helps the brain relax.

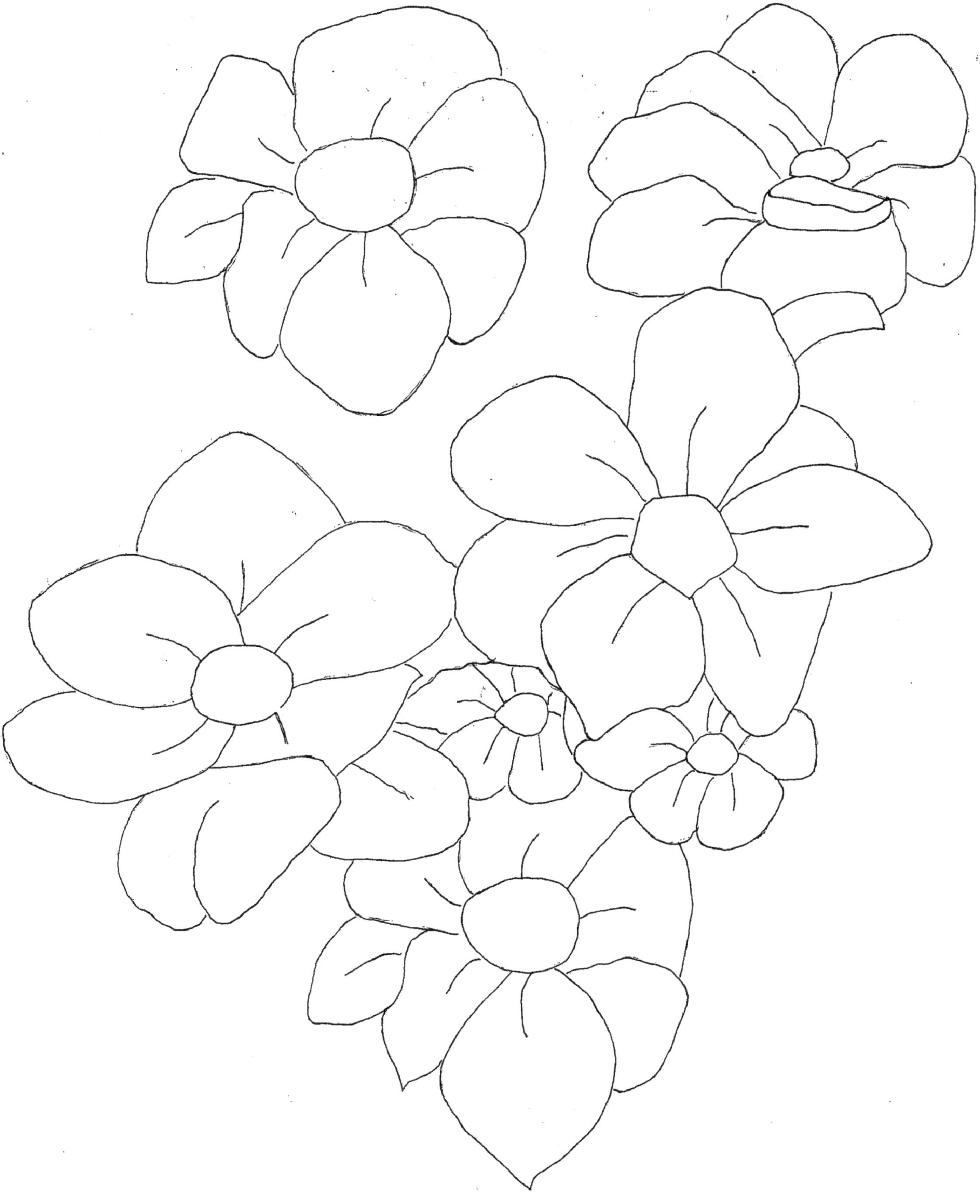

Relaxation reduces the fight or flight response.

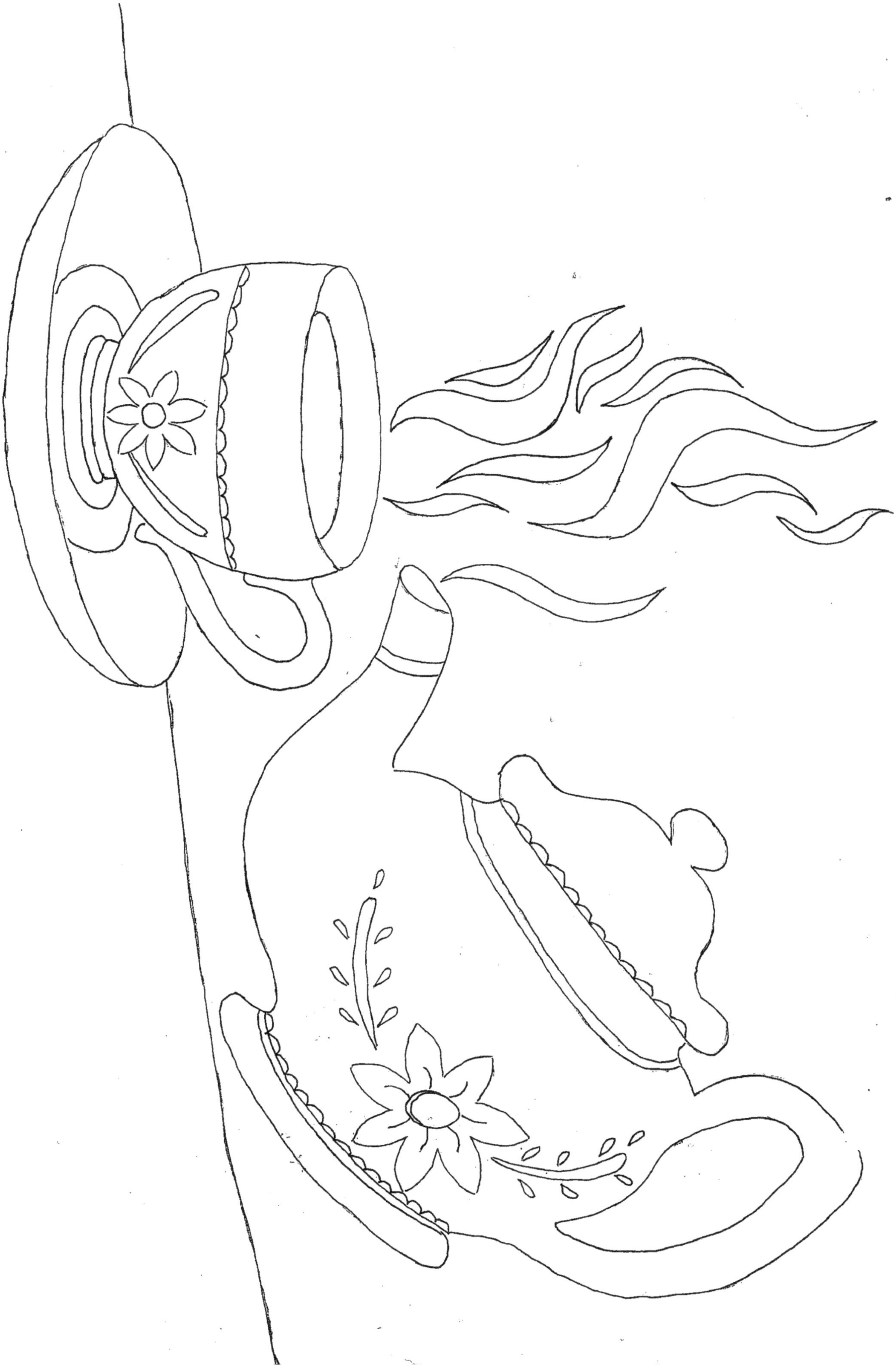

Relaxation can reduce the development of disease.

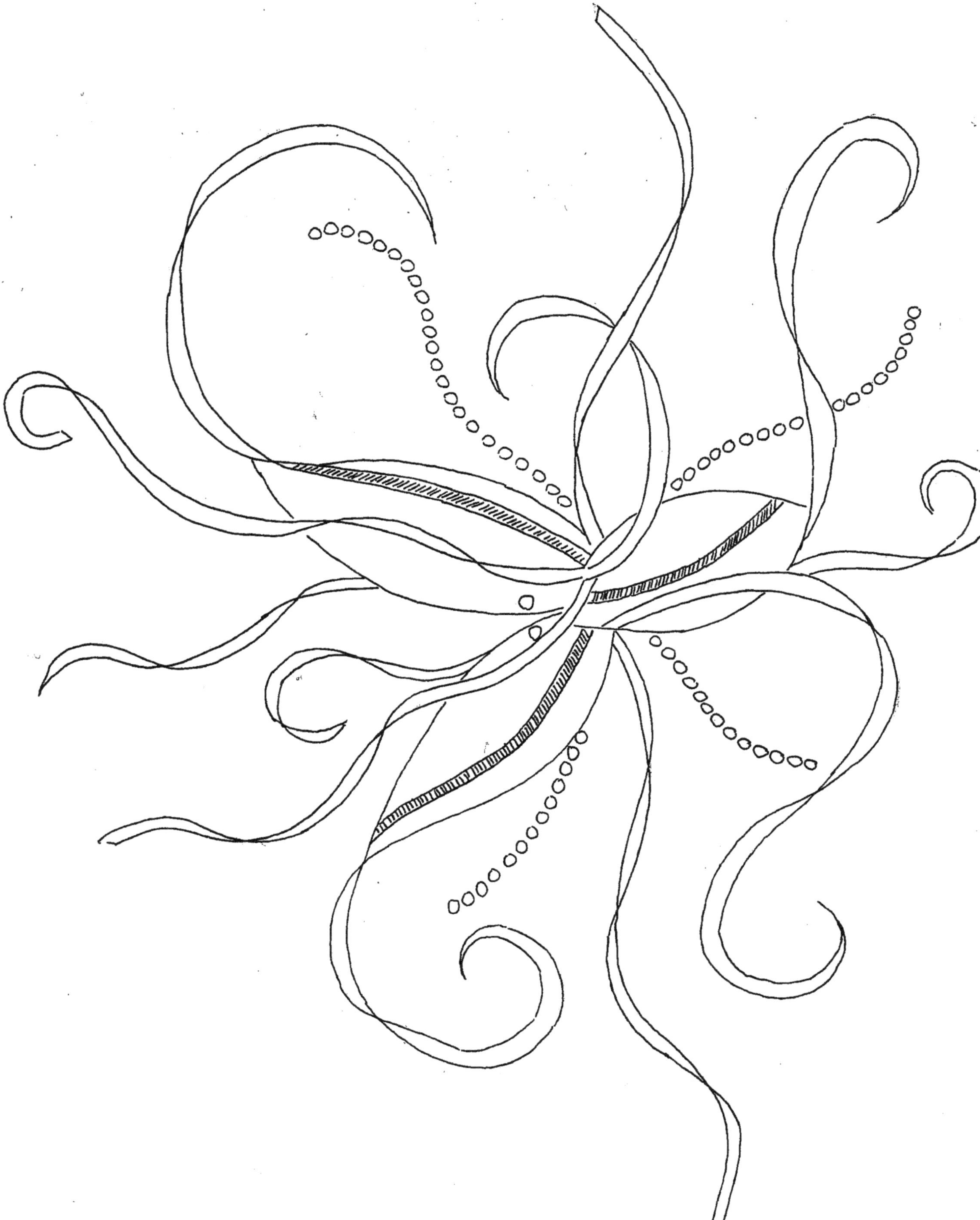

Relaxing helps you make better decisions.

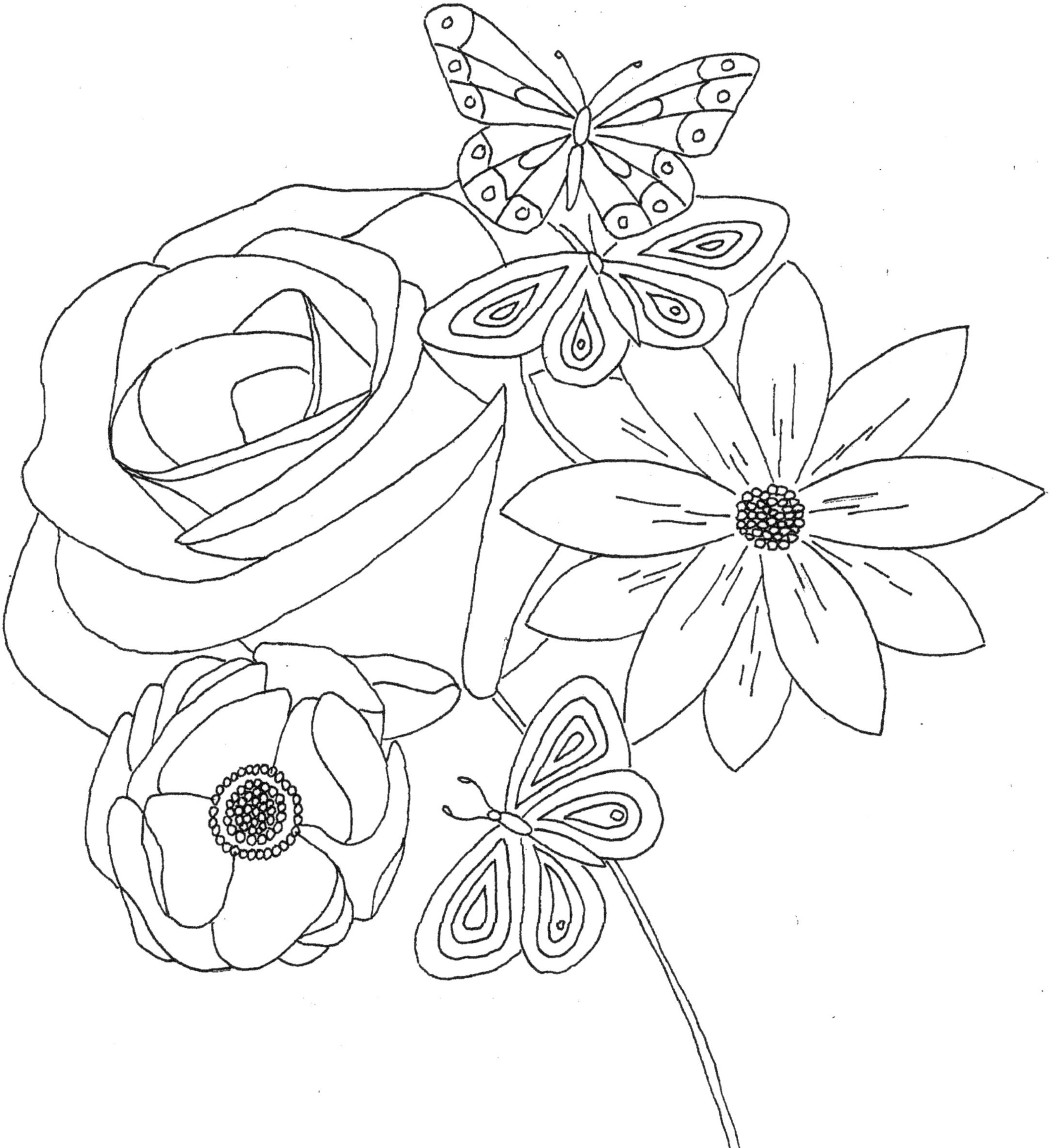

Relaxation increases the blood flow to the muscles.

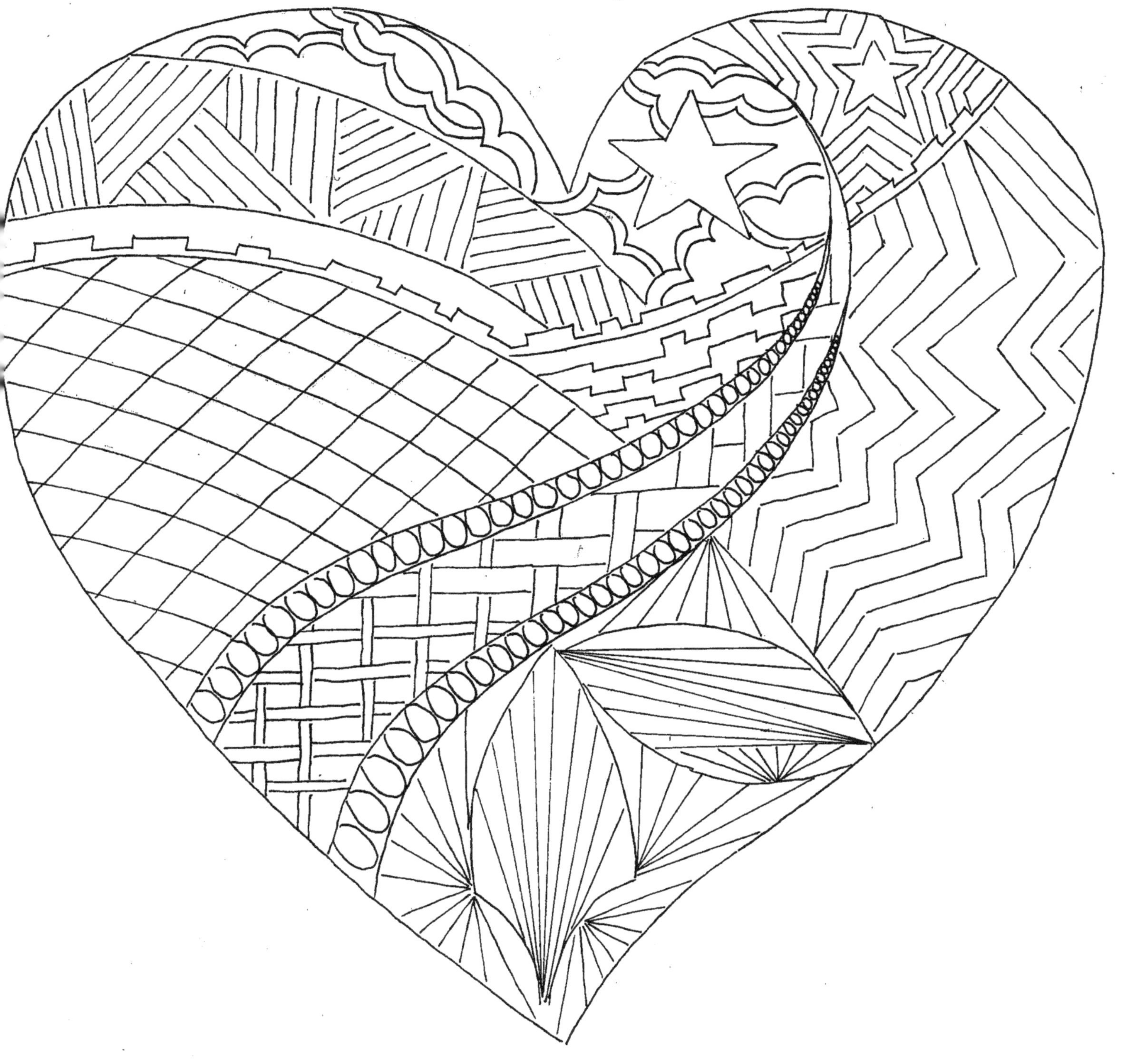

Relaxing keeps you safe from depression.

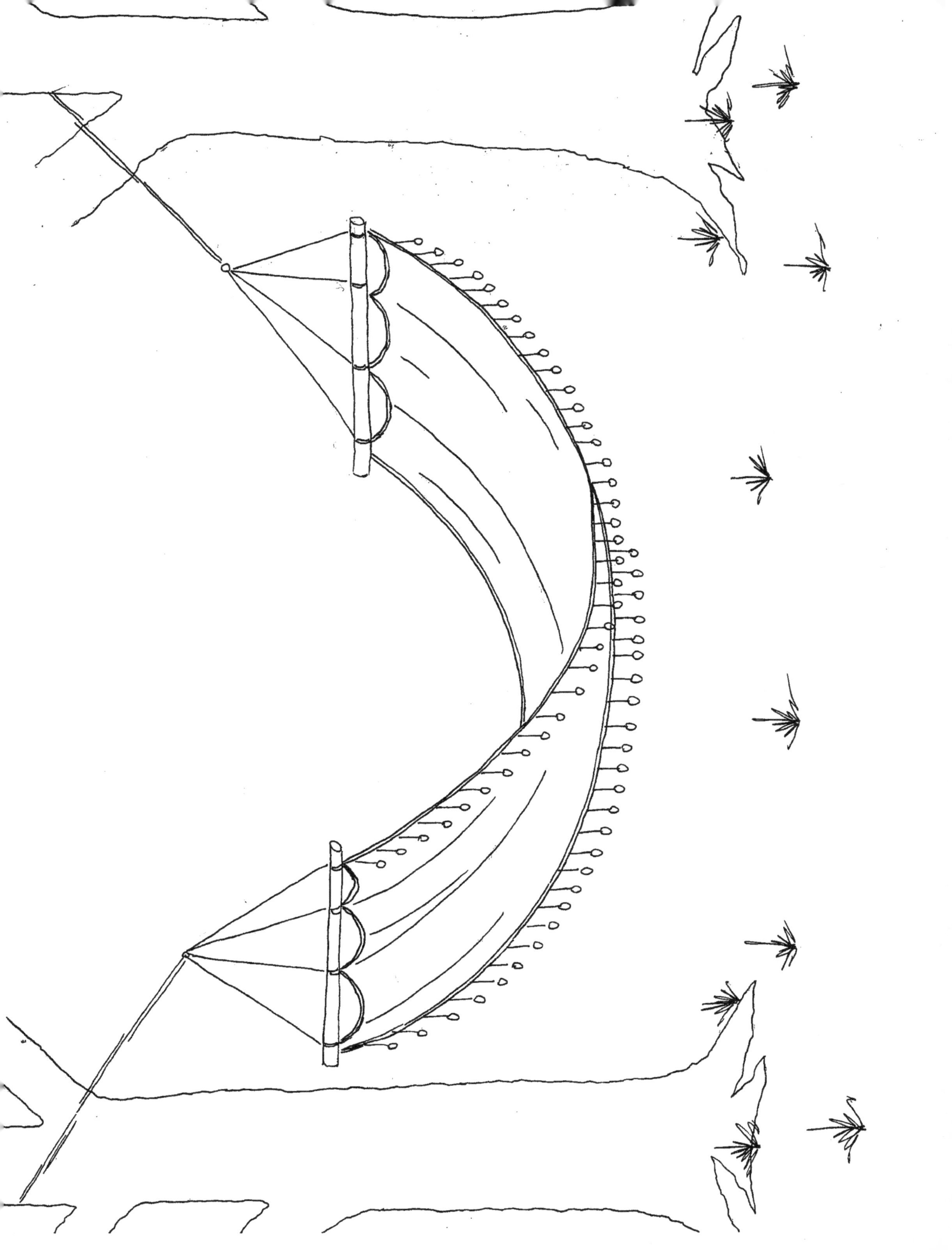

Relaxing lowers your risk for strokes.

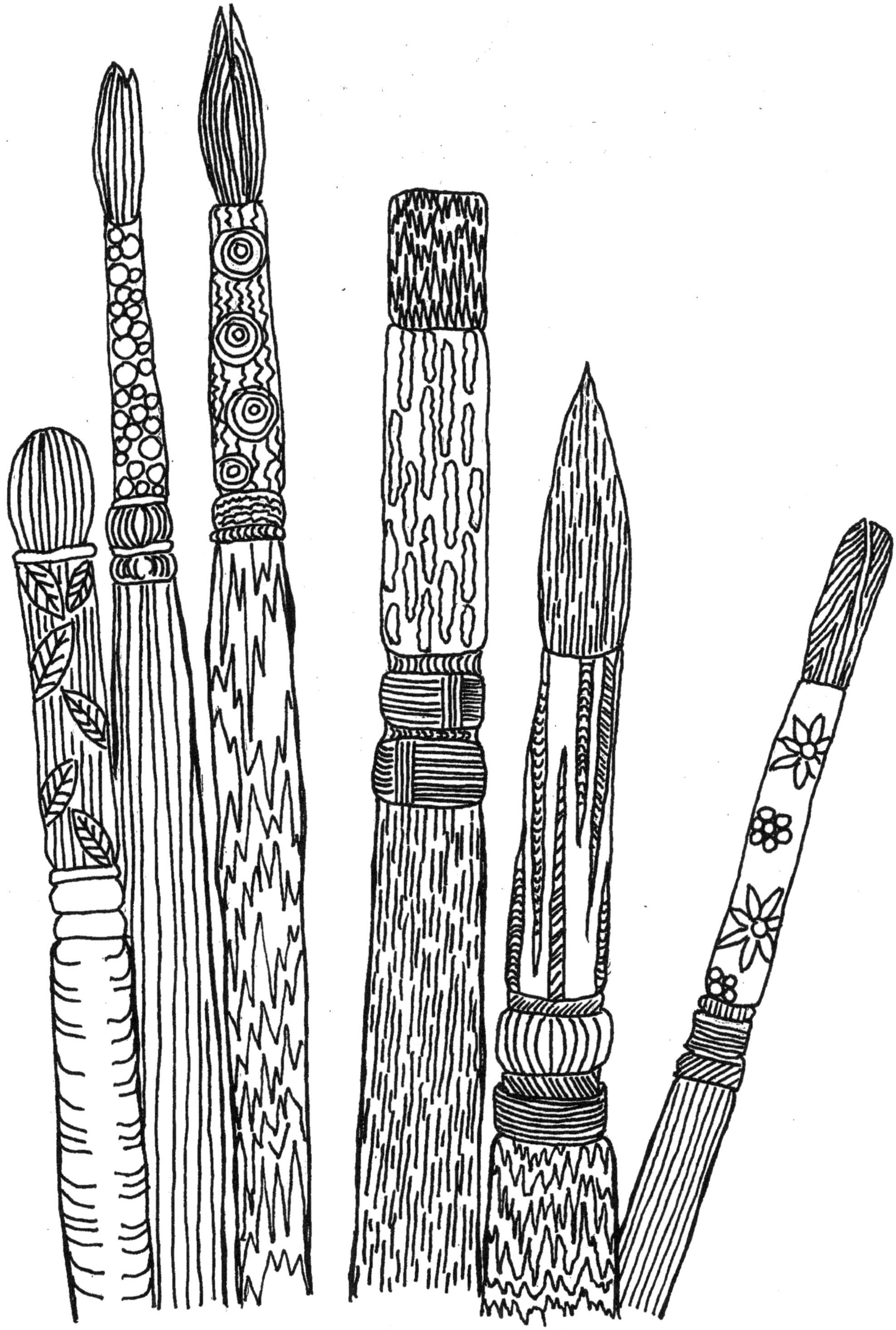

Relaxing protects your heart.

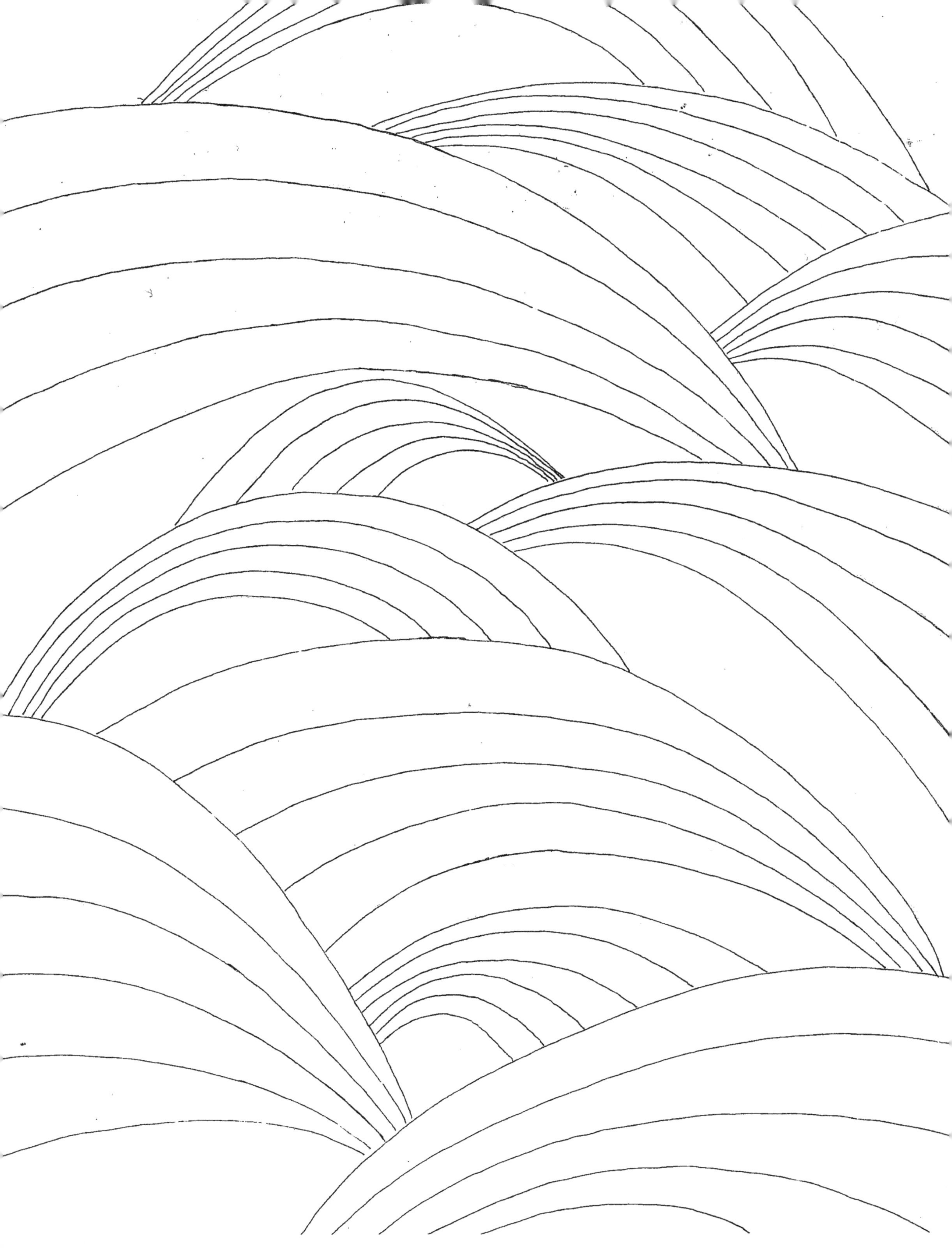

Laughter, even deliberately induced can be relaxing.

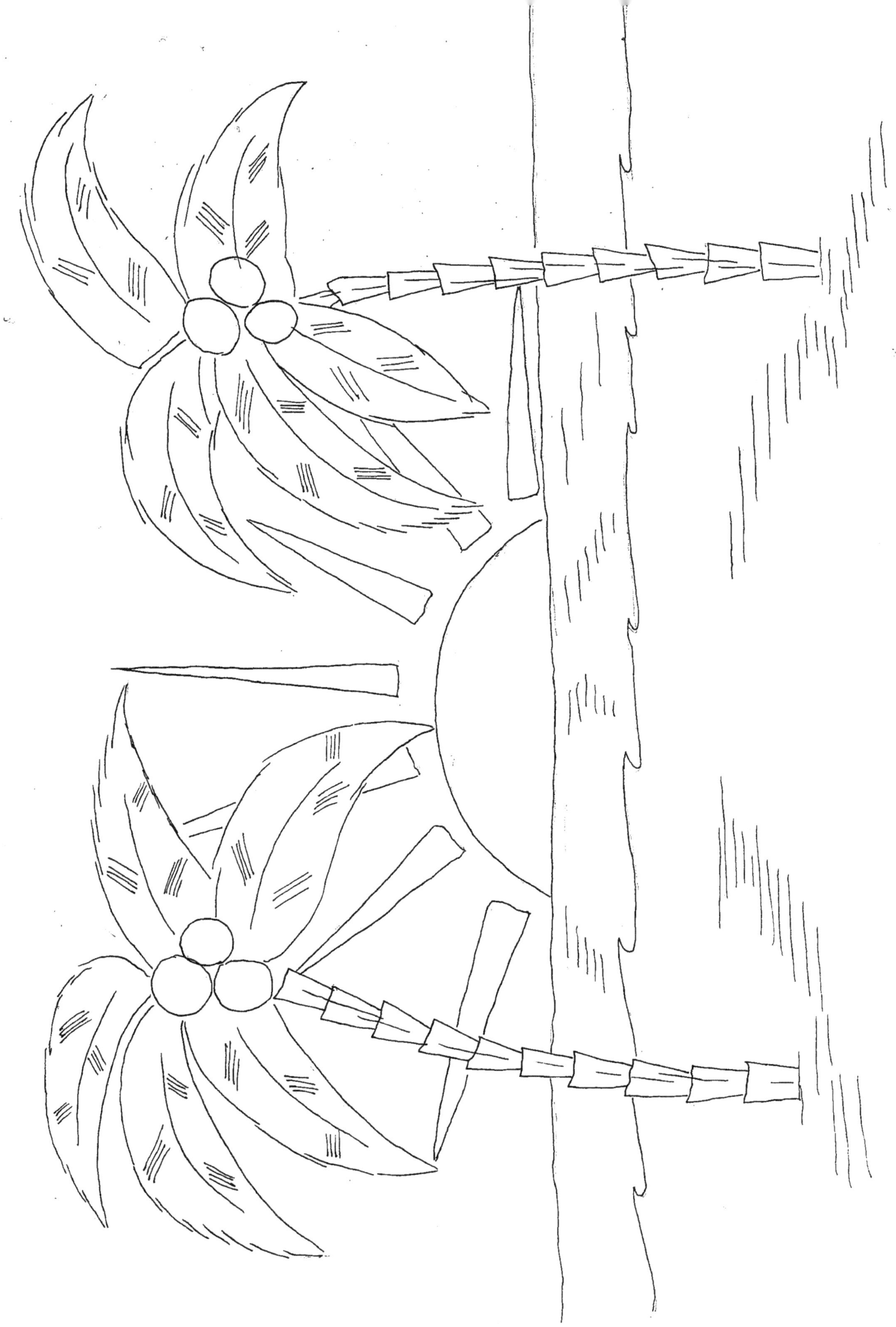

Relaxation is beneficial to our health.

Relaxation boosts the immune system.

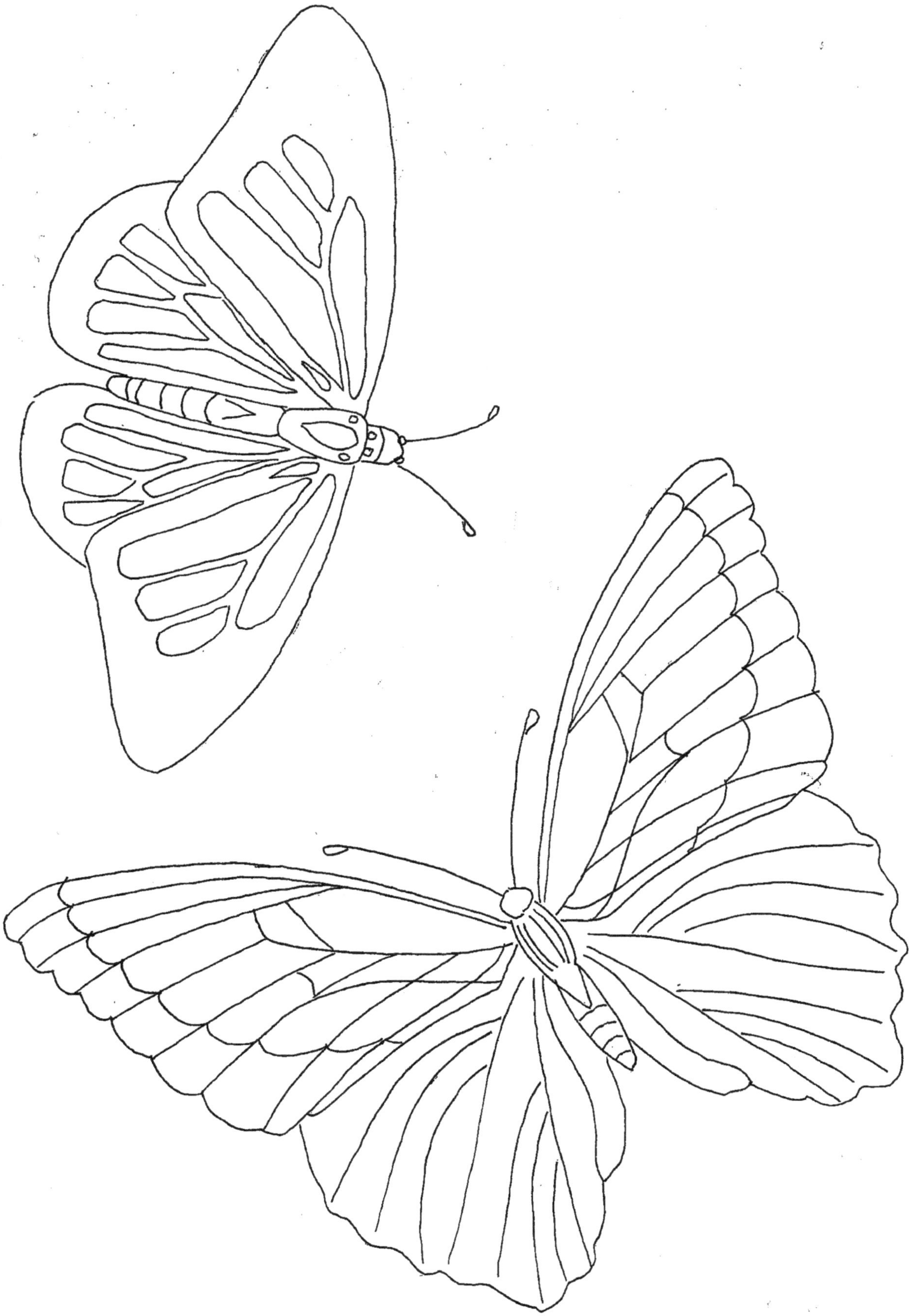

Breathe. Relax. Meditate.

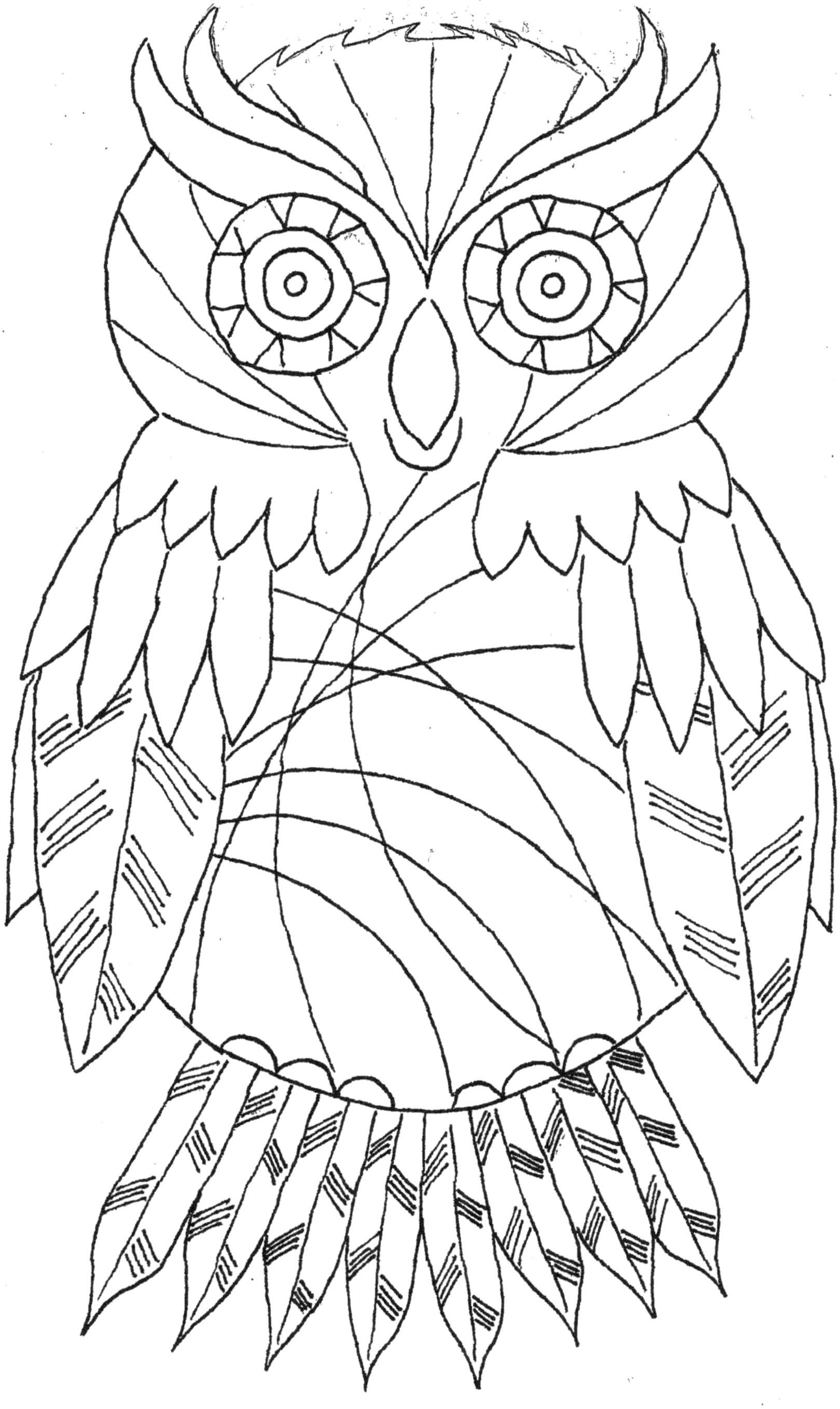

Find your inner peace.

Relax.

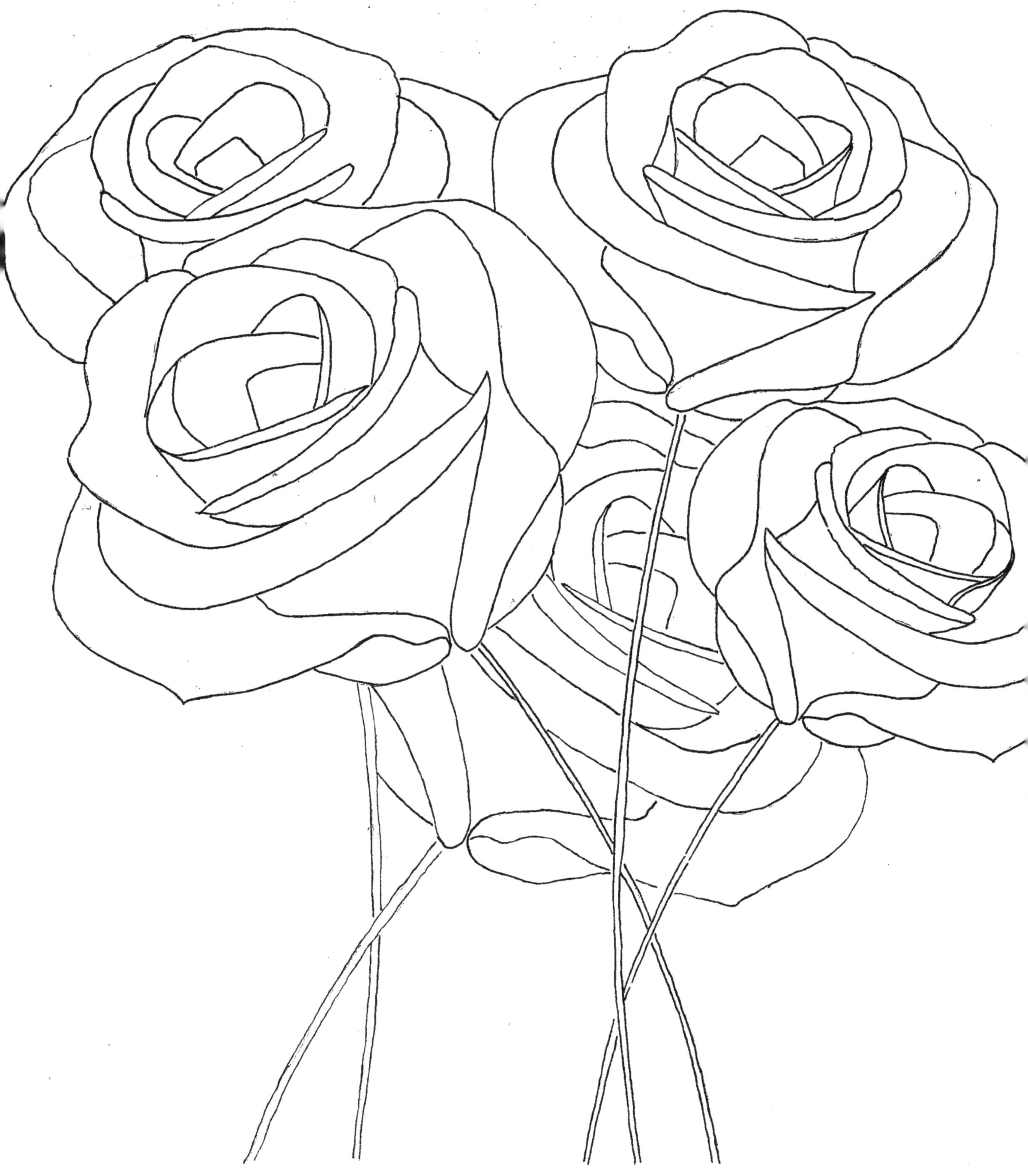

Relaxing eases acne.

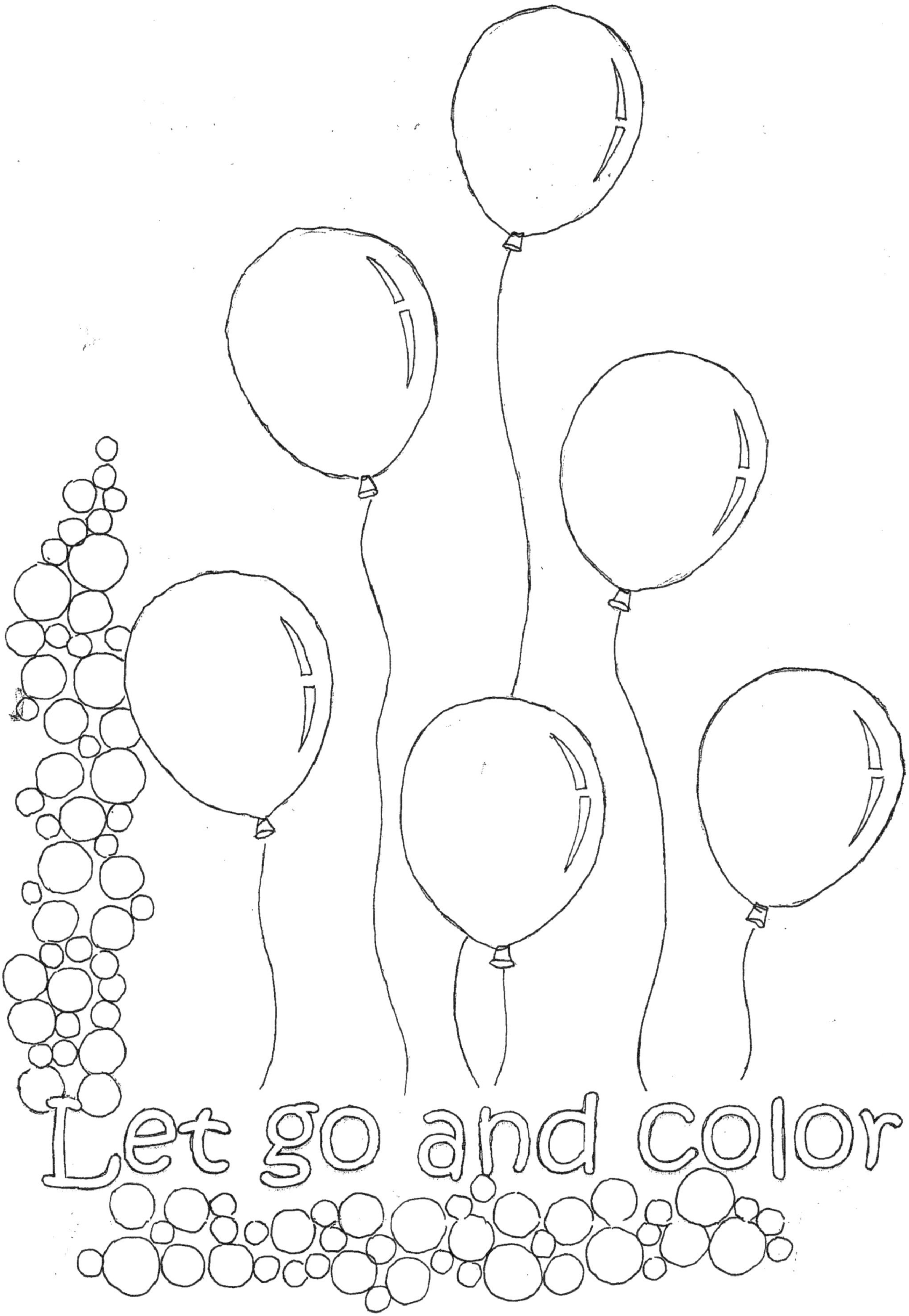
Let go and color

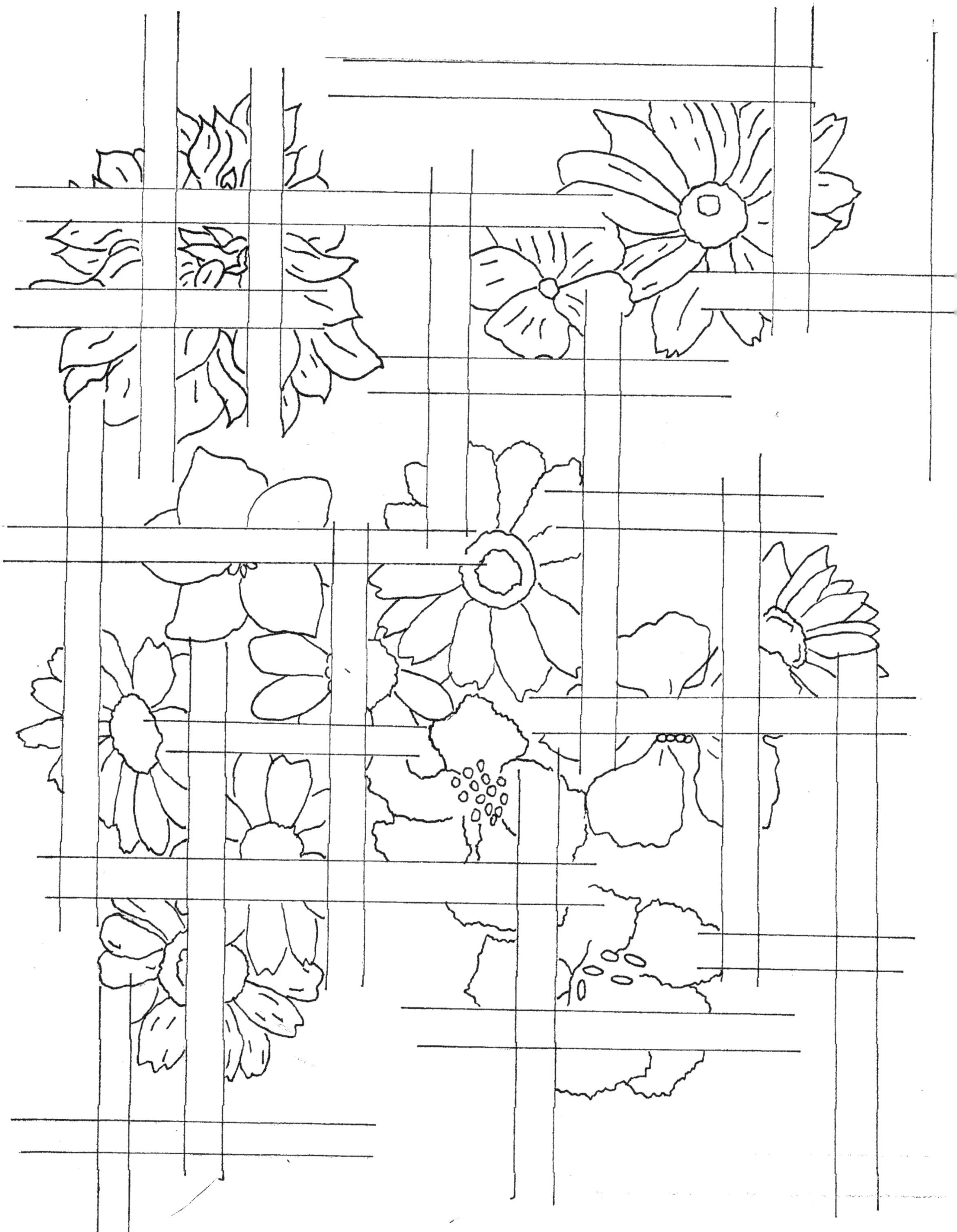

www.ingramcontent.com/pod-product-compliance
Lightning Source LLC
Chambersburg PA
CBHW080613190526
45169CB00007B/3002
9781523637973